Women, the Beauty of you!
The Way Men See You...

Clem Benton

authorHOUSE®

AuthorHouse™
1663 Liberty Drive, Suite 200
Bloomington, IN 47403
www.authorhouse.com
Phone: 1-800-839-8640

First published by AuthorHouse 4/7/2009

ISBN: 978-1-4389-6308-2 (sc)

Printed in the United States of America
Bloomington, Indiana

This book is printed on acid-free paper.

*Dedicated to Camille, my beautiful
daughter, who is so much like me.*

Acknowledgments

I would like to thank my brother and friend, Phillip Bouie, who was very inspirational and encouraging during this project. To Leslie Ross, who really believed in these poems and felt that I should share them with the world. To Sheila Shultz, an amazing and gifted woman who was my beacon and the driving force behind this project.

My mother, Gloria, and my stepmother, Carrie. Both of you have been inspirational to me over the years, and I have seen so much pure and deep beauty in you.

There are others who have inspired me beyond your imagination. You know who you are. Thank you so much for your belief and encouragement.

To Maureen, who has loved me unconditionally since the day we met. You are my queen! Thanks for always being there for me.

Thanks to God; without him, I can do nothing.

Contents

The Reason

I really want to share with women what men think of them from a man's perspective. Over the years, I've had many conversations with men, and it has amazed me, the things we think of women. Women are our inspiration in every area of life, even if some of us are not able to admit or show it.

Men are always thinking about sex. Yet, there is a tender side to a man, as you will see while reading "When Women Hurt" and "Women Sleeping."

One of my close female friends said that some women do not care what men think of them. I guess I had never thought of it like that. However, this book is my gift to the women who do care, as well as those who are curious. This is the way men see you in every area of life. It encompasses the things you do, how you look, what you wear, where you go, how you feel, and many more interesting things.

This book is intended to be funny, inspirational, and insightful. It is what men have thought, are thinking, and will always think of women.

This book is in no way meant to offend, degrade, or hurt anyone.

Enjoy!

The True Beauty of a Woman
Beauty, Strength, and Honor

The True Beauty of a Woman
Beauty, Strength, and Honor

There have been so many writings about the beauty of a woman, and I have decided to add "The True Beauty of a Woman" to the many great collections that exist.

As a little boy being raised by my mother, stepmother, grandmother, and aunt, I learned a lot about the beauty, strength, and honor of a woman when I was not even aware of what I was learning.

I wish I had some deep revelation to share with you regarding this poem. I don't. It's just what I've come up with watching how Mom, Carrie, Dear, and Daisy handled the challenges of life that they faced while raising their kids. Through the good, the bad, and the ugly, they were always there. Their beauty, strength, and honor always shone bright, even when they couldn't see their own way. They spoke words of life and peace and always carried a smile to get you through the day.

I believe many of you will identify with this poem in different ways. That's the beauty of it! Because somewhere in this poem I hope you can see your true beauty, strength, and honor.

Thank you for being you!

The True Beauty of a Woman
Beauty, Strength, and Honor

I desire to know you in your true beauty that lights every corner of the world.

I desire to know you in your true **strength** that holds all evil at bay.

I desire to know you in your true **honor** that the world has so graciously given you.

I desire to know you in your true **beauty** that discloses when you are troubled with the cares of life.

I desire to know you in your true **strength** that touches every broken heart that passes your way.

I desire to know you in your true **honor** that embraces every living soul and gives hope to all.

I desire to know you in the true **beauty** of your whispers that reach into the heart of every soul, sparking the fire of life.

I desire to know you in your true **strength** of encouragement that breaks the chains of bondage and despair.

I desire to know you in your true **honor** that has withstood the trials of life and healed many.

I desire to know you in your true quietness of **beauty** and the peace that it brings to all humanity.

I desire to know you in your true **strength** that has carried many to greatness and crowned them with excellence.

I desire to know you in your true **honor** that you have sacrificed for the love of life and the love of family.

I desire to know you in your true **beauty** and in the simplicity that you so willingly share.

I desire to know you in your true **strength** and in the simplicity that you so willingly give.

I desire to know you in your true **honor** and in the simplicity with which you so willingly bless others.

I desire to know you, plain and simple, in the true beauty, strength, and honor that you are.

Why Men Look at Women

Why Men Look at Women

It is natural for men to look at women. It is who we are and what we enjoy doing. Women have such a powerful effect on us, and it is amazing to witness that effect. Some men are still not sure about, or do not understand, the effect that a woman has on them. They feel guilty looking at or admiring women. They feel as if they are doing something wrong or that they are cheating. However, no matter how they feel, they will still look. Men look at women because it is a part of our DNA. There is something beautiful about every woman, which compels us to look. It is not mystical or magical; it is simply *The Beauty of You!*

Types of Lookers

The three types of men lookers are

The Bold: They do not care who they are with or where they are. If they see a woman who is attractive, they are going to look. I believe everyone knows who this guy is!

The Groupie: These are the men who get with their friends, and all they do is look at women, talk about them, and make comments to them that they would not make if they were alone. I believe every man has fit or will fit into this category at one time or another.

The Shy: These are the men who really enjoy looking at women but don't want anyone else to know that they are lookers. These are the men most people would not think are lookers. Women who think their men are not interested in other women are most likely involved with shy ones.

Why Men Look at Women

Because of the way you walk, your tantalizing smile, and your beautiful and sexy style.
Because when you stop, what we see in you makes us want to drop, drop so low; at times we don't know where to go.
Because when you sit, we always look for your slit, which makes us say, "We will delay the rest of the day!"

Because when you stand, we see why you're in demand.
Because the way your clothes fit, it makes us want to sit.
Because when you move, it makes everything around you shift to your groove.
That's when we stand and say, "Man, I've got to have a fan!"
Because when you bend, you don't seem to notice all the men.
We are sweatin' like dogs, ready to leap like frogs.

Because when you straighten up, you make all of us wake up.
You stopped us from leaping to what we thought was our beacon.
Because when you move, you do it so smooth; we stand in awe, as if we just broke our jaw.
Because when you look at us, the gleam of your beam touches us to the extreme and makes us want to scream.

Because you want to know why we seem so confused at the way you move, and are willing to give all just for you to call.
Because without you, we honestly don't know what to do, so we chase after you until you give us a clue.
Now that you know, you mesmerize us to the core, and the way you are simply elevates us to the next bar.

When Women Hurt

When Women Hurt

This reaches into the heart of a man and shows his tender side. Whether a man is able to show that he cares (many are not), there is something deep down inside of him that hates to see women hurt. He may or may not have been the cause of their pain; however, if he was, he may lack the skills to express his remorse. I am not making excuses for men, but I am sharing with you the reality of life through a man's eyes. Men do care when women hurt, more than anyone can imagine and more than they may be able to express.

When women are hurt, sad, or weeping, at times we don't know what to do.

The Hurting Ones

The three types of hurting women are

The Outburst: The women who cry aloud, don't control their emotions, and are very vocal about their feelings. A lot of men will run away from or avoid this type because they feel it's too much drama. If you are trying to get the attention of a man, it is a good idea to know what kind of show of emotions will touch his heart.

The Withdrawal: The women who grow quiet, withdraw themselves, and may even shed a few tears. These women are most likely to get the attention they need. Personally, I think this is the most affective method to the heart of a man. A man does not like to feel that a woman has withdrawn her emotions from him. However, we are all different, so some men may react better to the first and third types of women.

The Tough One: The women who appear as if they don't ever get hurt. They won't admit or show when they are hurt. Many men treat this type with disrespect or are callus toward the women's feelings. Men might think, "Well, she doesn't care. Nothing bothers her anyway."

When Women Hurt

At times when you **hurt,** it seems as if you are no longer alert.
Just so you know, we hurt too, but at times we don't know what to do.
At times when you are **sad,** we don't like it because we can't be glad.
When you are sad, we desire only to carry your bag.
At times when you **weep,** it seems as if our world grows bleak.
Because when you don't weep, our whole world is at its peak.

At times when you **hurt,** we know it's over some stupid dirt.
Maybe even ours, but trust me, we don't mean to make you sour.
At times when you are **sad,** we don't like it, because for us that's really bad.
At times when you **weep,** we want to gladly take the heat, to make you smile, and to blow away all of your clouds.

At times when you **hurt,** our world turns into nothing but dirt.
At times when you are **sad,** we miss your power, which gets us through the hour.
At times when you **weep,** we hate it because our world turns in to a swirl.

At times when you **hurt,** we really, really do care, and only wish that we could take all of your pain to bear.
At times when you are **sad,** all we can think of is how to make you glad.
At times when you **weep,** all we want to do is bend our knee and say to you, "Baby, no more worries, because you and me can surely make it be."
We know at times it's tough, but our desire is to carry you through the rough.
For we love you dear, and desire only to hold you near.

Women at the Club

Women at the Club

Every man has seen a woman at the club who stays in his mind for weeks to come. The club is a place where men go to see every *style* of woman. The exciting part about the club is you do not know where all the women come from. They could be local, from out of town, or from another country.

There is something magnetic about a woman who can go to the club, be herself, and have fun. That is very attractive to a man. If you notice, she is the one most guys are trying to dance or talk with. She is the one that puts a man at ease. She is in control, and everyone knows it.

Styles of Women at the Club

The three styles of women at the club are

The Sexy One: She is the one who walks with confidence, knows what she is wearing looks sexy on her, and moves with grace and class. She is the one that is watched by everyone, and no one can miss that she is there.

The Shy One: She is quiet, yet powerful. She is not aware there is something desirable and mysterious about her. She is the one men really want to know because they believe there is a tiger hidden underneath her shyness. Men desire to tame that tiger, and, if they can't, they sure would like to try.

The Loud One: We all know her. She is the one who is saying with her actions, "Look at me; I want everyone to notice me!" She is very vocal, possibly drunk, and moves all over the club seeking attention. Most men will avoid her like the plague.

Women at the Club

Never have we seen so many sexy women on the scene who are so alive
and ready to bump with us on the side.
We try to be cool, the way men do, until we see you and break down
without a clue.
The sexy things you wear, showing off what you bear to us brothers just
isn't fair.

Because for us men, we don't understand when you get down with the
band and leave us at the beer stand.
When we see the beauty of your sexiness and the way you move to the
groove, it blows our minds, and takes us weeks to shake your heat.
It seems at times that you know you have power to drive us, from hour to
hour, only to make us bow down and cower.

You party all through the night, just to leave at the sight of light.
You leave the scene, like a precious queen.
We stand there and look like we've just been took, feeling all ashamed,
as if you were to blame.
We manage to make it home, just to sleep all alone, wondering what
we'll say to the homeboys the very next day.

We think of some line to rap about in time.
We talk about the one who got away and pray to God that someday
she'll pass our way.
All the men say they understand the way, because it seems to happen
every day.
As we prepare to go out at night, thinking about the beauties that will be
in our sight.
We try to be cool, the way men do, until we see you and break down
without a clue.

You Conceived

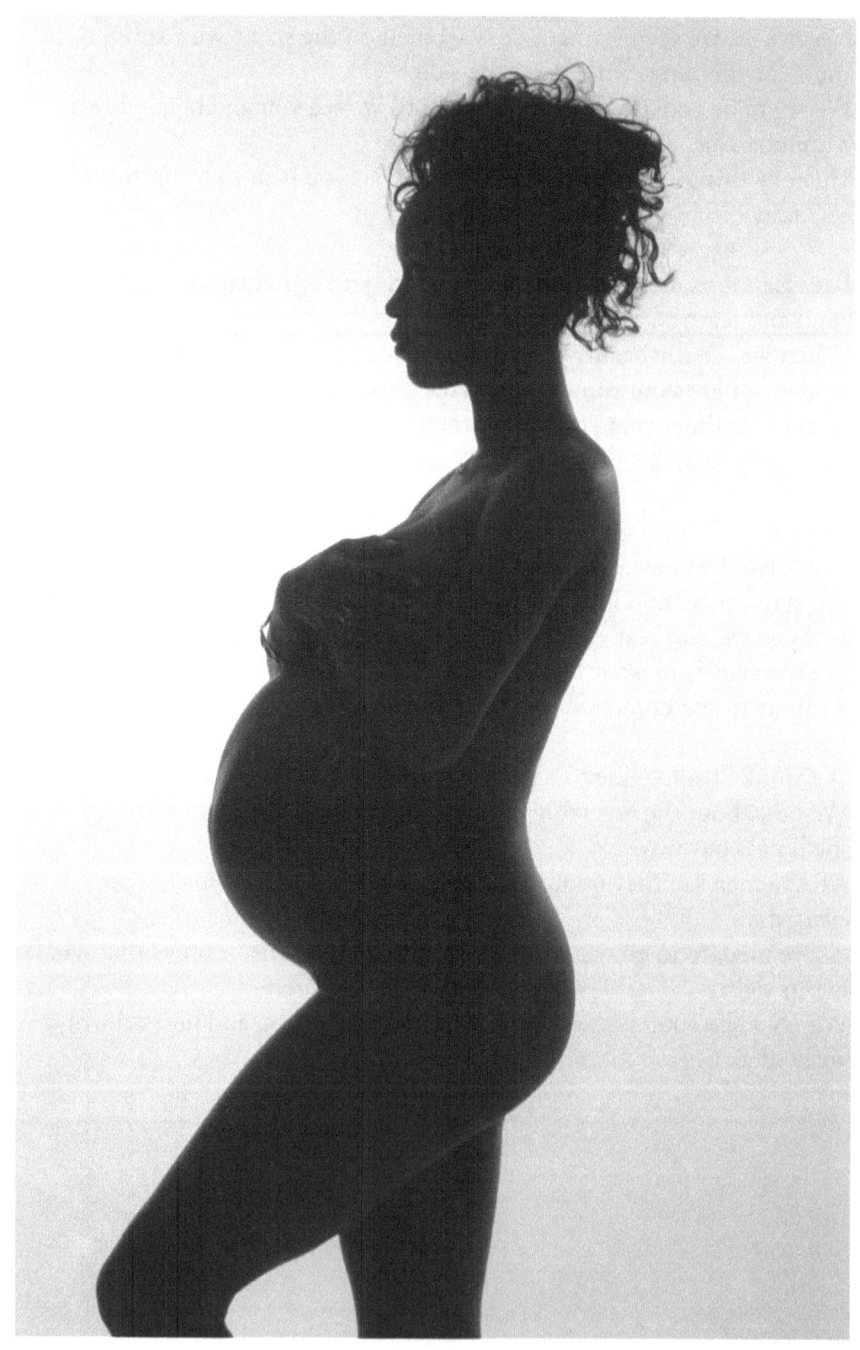

You Conceived

What can I say? The beauty of a pregnant woman is astonishing! It is a miracle that she can bring life into a world that is in so much pain.

A pregnant woman's mind is multifaceted as she searches for ways to protect the child and give him or her a good life. She wants to be the best she can be for the person she will give birth to. She starts to glow with beauty from the depth of her soul, a beauty so deep only a pregnant woman knows.

As her body changes and she starts to show, notice how her beauty attracts others who want to share in her joy.

The child is here and what great cheer! Yet, this is just the beginning of her nurturing process and all her dreams of what her child will be.

Pregnant Women

The three categories of pregnant women are

The Sure One: She is the one most men are attracted to. She keeps herself looking good throughout her pregnancy. She dresses well, she smiles, she still has a spring in her step, and she feels good about herself. This woman can have any man she wants even if she is pregnant. Men *really* desire her and she knows it. This one has probably kept herself in shape before her pregnancy, and will continue to do so during and after it, too.

The Unsure one: She appears to be unsure of how people perceive her. She thinks she is not attractive and will not make eye contact with others, especially men. She walks with doubt and everyone can see it. She does not recognize her own beauty, and if someone compliments her, she will not receive it. She is the one men would love to give a smile or word of encouragement to if given the opportunity.

The Hating One: She is the one who hates that she is pregnant. She cannot believe this has happened to her. She is frustrated and is not sure what she will do with her child. Nothing else need be said.

You Conceived!

The moment you conceived, you knew it, for the joy of life pierced your soul with so much excitement!
Excitement! Yes! To be all you can be for that which you have conceived!
You are excited! For you have received a blessing of life, indeed for a price!

You are showing now! And the world only sees a glimpse of that which you have conceived.
You are glowing now! All can see that you are proud of that which you have conceived.
Many notice you, many approach you, and they only want to share with you that which you have conceived.

Your child is here and what great cheer! For the life that you conceived will begin to receive!
Your child is here, and the blessing you crave that the child may be brave! Brave in wisdom and insight that she may see through the night! For that which you have conceived is really all right!
Your child is here, but nine months ago not as near! Conceived in passion, maybe through some midnight action.

Your child develops a life of her own and chases a destiny only she can condone! That which you conceived may someday begin to breed!
Your child whom you conceived has thought about great deeds! Great potential to possess in order to help others reach their best!
You have nurtured, taught, and trained that which you conceived, only to allow the world to have your seed! With joy and pain you brought forth a great gain to give to a world that is in so much pain.

Women Who Ride the Bus

Women Who Ride the Bus

There are always these questions in a man's mind: "Where is she from? Where is she going? Where does she work and what does she do? Will she talk to me? Can I get to know her? Why she is riding the bus?" The questions may continue, depending on the man.

There is something thrilling and motivating about women who ride the bus. They seem to be in a class of their own. This poem is from the prospective of working men and women who cross paths daily on the bus or bus route and the excitement that women bring to the men who see them.

Thrilling Women Who Ride the Bus

The three types of thrilling women are

The Fashion Beauty: She comes every day looking exceptional. There is something soothing about her presence. She is the one that motivates and inspires men to get through their day. If she is not at the bus stop or not riding the bus, she is greatly missed. She is the one that every man hopes to sit by, share a conversation with, and get to know. Her beauty is electrifying and she is very desirable!

The Casual One: She always looks nice. She is friendly and warm, and she smiles. Men like her, and some even admire her. She is easy to talk with, encouraging, and trustworthy. She makes you want to share your joy and pains with her. Men may not desire her at first, but over time she will steal their hearts and have them craving her company every day. One day they'll wake up and be in love with her. Men, be careful with this one!

The Stale One: She is there every day, but her spirit says to everyone, "Leave me alone; I don't want to be bothered! Men, don't even think about it!" We wonder what happened to you. We feel bad for you because you seem to be distant and disconnected from yourself. We feel bad for you, and, if you would allow us, we would try to cheer you up. We wonder if you have been hurt by one of us.

Women Who Ride the Bus

In the morning, we stand in awe at all the diverse beauties there are.
We see you at the bus stop and on the bus too. We see where you get off
to do what you do.
Every morning, because of you, we all have a lot of pep in our step.

You may never know what you do that encourages us to get through.
We get on the bus and look for you too.
Out of all the beauties, we have a special one too.
We may or may not talk; you may or may not know, but for us, you are
the gust that gets us on and off that bus.

We notice all of you, from head to toe.
Yes, all of you, even if you may not know.
We love the way you smell, and your outfits we know very well.
Your nails, lipstick, and hair, we notice that you keep so fair.
Your shoes too, and how they bring you pride to jumpstart your stride.

We know that some of you know the inspiration we draw from you as we
pass through.
Our hearts are pumping, we both know, while we're contemplating
which way to go.
We feel the power of the connection, even as we turn in another
direction.

In the morning, we'll stand in awe at all the diverse beauties there are.

Tall Women

It's no secret that men admire and desire tall women for various reasons. One of those reasons is their long legs. We love the long legs; we seek and search you out because we want to know what you're all about.

Years ago, tall women appeared to by shy, withdrawn, and embarrassed by their height. Today many of them seem confident, appreciated, desired, and loved. You are indeed desired by the men who worship you.

The three types of tall women are

The Confident and Desired One: She is bold and sexy! She wears heels to enhance her height. She is confident that she looks good, and she knows that she is desired by men. She is the one that everyone looks at and compliments when she graces the world with her presence. She smiles and walks with pride, yet she is friendly and approachable. She puts everyone at ease, and she seems to hold the world in the palm of her hand.

The Appreciated One: She accepts that she is tall and appreciates who she is as a person, but she has not completely embraced her height as a power, as a force, or as sexy and desirable. If you tell her that she is sexy and desirable, it may be hard for her to accept. She will most likely say, "Well, I don't really see myself like that. But thanks!"

The Loved one: She has an inner beauty that compels you to befriend her. She is not going to dress sexy or nice. She wears jeans to hide her long legs. Perhaps she doesn't have confidence that she looks good or ever will. You have to love her as a person because she is pure. No matter who you are or where you're from, you will like this one. She is a hidden gem! What if she truly understood this?

Tall Women

Back in the day you refused to come out and play.
You hid inside and sat on your backside.
You were so shy, you just waved to us good-bye.
Now time has passed, and you're a beauty with so much class.
We seek you out because we're dying to know what you're all about.

All our fantasies have you there.
We've been waiting and waiting for you to take us there.
We watch the way you move and have never seen a lady so smooth.
We lie down and say, "She just blew me away!"
When you're around, all eyes are on your crown, for now you rule, and
we love that you do it so cool.

We love you walking in heels; it makes us want to run on the treadmill.
We love you in a skirt, because our imagination runs behind you and
make us wanna lurk.
We love it when you stop, because we like the feel of you ringing our
clock.

Now you should know, most of us men really want to win with you again
and again.
Now that you'll come out to play, when you pass our way, please give us
some time in your day.
Now that you know you're part of the elite three or four, make us proud
and stick around for a while.

Our Women in Law Enforcement!

Our Women in Law Enforcement!

Many men would love to know you. We would love to know what drives you, what gives you the desire to fight crime and put your life on the line every day. We want to know your background, your passions, and what you do away from the job. You are and will always be a mystery to us.

When you stop us, as you approach our vehicle, we may be somewhat nervous but excited too. We want to know if you will flirt with us, or will you be all business. We don't even mind getting a ticket from you if you will just be nice and give us a smile.

When you are respectful and smile, most of the time you can get us to do whatever you ask even if it's to get in the backseat of your cruiser with your handcuffs on our wrists.

With all due respect, we understand what you've been through to get where you are. We know it's not an easy job, and deep down inside of us, we admire what you do—giving of yourself so freely to help so many that are needy.

You are the force that balances the system. We thank you and want you to know that you are loved!

Our Women in Law Enforcement

Oh, how we know what it must have meant for you to be accepted in law enforcement as your first stint!
The odds were against you from the start, since many didn't want you in law enforcement—not any part.
But you knew in your heart that in law enforcement, you had a part, so you fought and won the right to carry your gun.

Our women in law enforcement have paved the way. That will make many have a better day!
Where would the world be without your fight? I know! Many would be without their light!
Because of your fight, wisdom, and precious insight, law enforcement has welcomed you with great delight!

We know it hasn't been easy, but instead, rough and tough and sometimes very queasy!
You fought with dignity and pride, but look at you now with so many at your side!
You have set the standard, which no person alone can handle! That if you have a desire, jump right in, and push, push, push until you win!

So right now, we put everything else aside, just to honor you for all the great things you do! Know that you are loved!

When You Sleep

When You Sleep

When you sleep, it brings out the protective side of a man. There is something on the inside of a man that makes him feel good about protecting his woman. He is protecting his prize; he is king!

There is a sexual excitement as well, knowing that he can go in a take a look at his woman while she is sleeping. Pulling the covers back and taking a look while you are sleeping is breathtaking to a man. That is why he comes to bed sometimes while you are sleep and initiates intimacy. He may pull those covers back and look at you, which causes him to desire you at that moment. We all know that men are visual. Men love to look! It is thrilling for him to watch you while you are sleeping.

Ask your man if he has ever pulled the covers back and watched you while you where sleeping. Ask him how it made him feel. If he is open and honest with you, you will see a side to him you didn't know existed.

The three types of women sleepers are

The Nude One: This woman is open and free with her body. She likes the idea of being naked in her bed and with the one she sleeps with. This is probably the favorite one for men. You are there with no restriction! That is exciting!

The Clothed One: This woman may not be comfortable with her body. She is boring and not sure of herself. There is no reason for a man to look under the covers. He sees her in her clothes all the time. She is boring!

The Lingerie One: What can a man say? Sleeping in lingerie is definitely sexy! We may not want it all the time, but every now and then it will blow us away. It will get our attention, and you will be in control! Nothing more need be said!

When You Sleep

Men love it when you **sleep** because we can watch the sexy way you lie.
Men love it when you **sleep** because we call all our boys to stand guard around the yard.
Men love it when you **sleep** because we get to stand tall and guard all of the halls and walls.

Men love it when you **sleep** because we come alive at the thought of protecting our prize.
Men love it when you **sleep** because we get to make you safe so we can take our place.
Men love it when you **sleep** because soon we know we will be next to your heat.

Men love it when you **sleep** because when we lie next to your body, it makes us very hardy.
Men love it when you **sleep** because all day we are hardy, knowing that at night we will be snuggling with you so tight.
Men love it when you **sleep** because we love to spy on your body that makes us so high.

Men love it when you **sleep** because we like to turn on the light and sneak a peek at your cheek.
Men love it when you **sleep** because as we look at you lying there so neat, we start to feel our own body heat.
Men love it when you **sleep** because we like to sing about the joy you bring to our boys, and then we all sing aloud with some noise.

Men love it when you **sleep** because now it's time for us to unwind, so we run to the bed, just to lie next to your head.
Men love it when you **sleep** because when we get in bed, time speeds ahead.
Men love it when you **sleep** because when time speeds ahead, we know before long we will be in bed lying next to you wrapped up in threads.

Your Light Shines!

Your Light Shines!

This shows the admiration, inspiration, insight, love, and passion from the heart of men regarding women in general. Without women, men would be in total darkness. We need, hunger and thirst after your light that you shine every day. Your presence provides hope, inspiration, and direction.

You may never know the inspiration that you provide to the world. We may never tell you what we really feel or think about you. You may never know the power of your smile, your touch, your advice, and your warmth. You may never know that men long to tell you that you are amazing. You may never know the peace and encouragement you bring with your very presence. You may never know that we appreciate you from our very core.

I hope that you are encouraged and inspired! I speak as one, but for all of us, our request to you is "Keep your light shining! We love and need you!"

Your Light Shines!

Woman! Because of you, the day will break!
Woman! The moment your feet touched the ground, the world slowed down.
Woman! Your first step of the day made Heaven's gates roll away.

Woman! As you showered, the angels released their power to guide you through another day secure.
Woman! As you dressed, the angles went west.
Woman! As you eat, the world waits at your gate to see your light, which always kills the night.

Woman! You left for the day, after holding the world at bay.
Woman! You displayed your light that gave all their sight.
Woman! You walked through the day, holding darkness at bay; you shared your beauty that inspired many to continue their duty.
Woman! Your day is ending, we all know, because it's getting windy.

Woman! You start for home, once again to allow darkness to roam.
Woman! You approach your gate, and there they all wait for you to pray the close of another day.
Woman! As you pray, the angels return from their stay.
They look at you and say, "Thanks for another precious day."

Woman! You are home now, and Heaven's gates have relocated
Heaven's gates await your command, to open again so life can expand.
Woman! You close another day as you lie, only to return and perform another excellent run.

Women Nurses

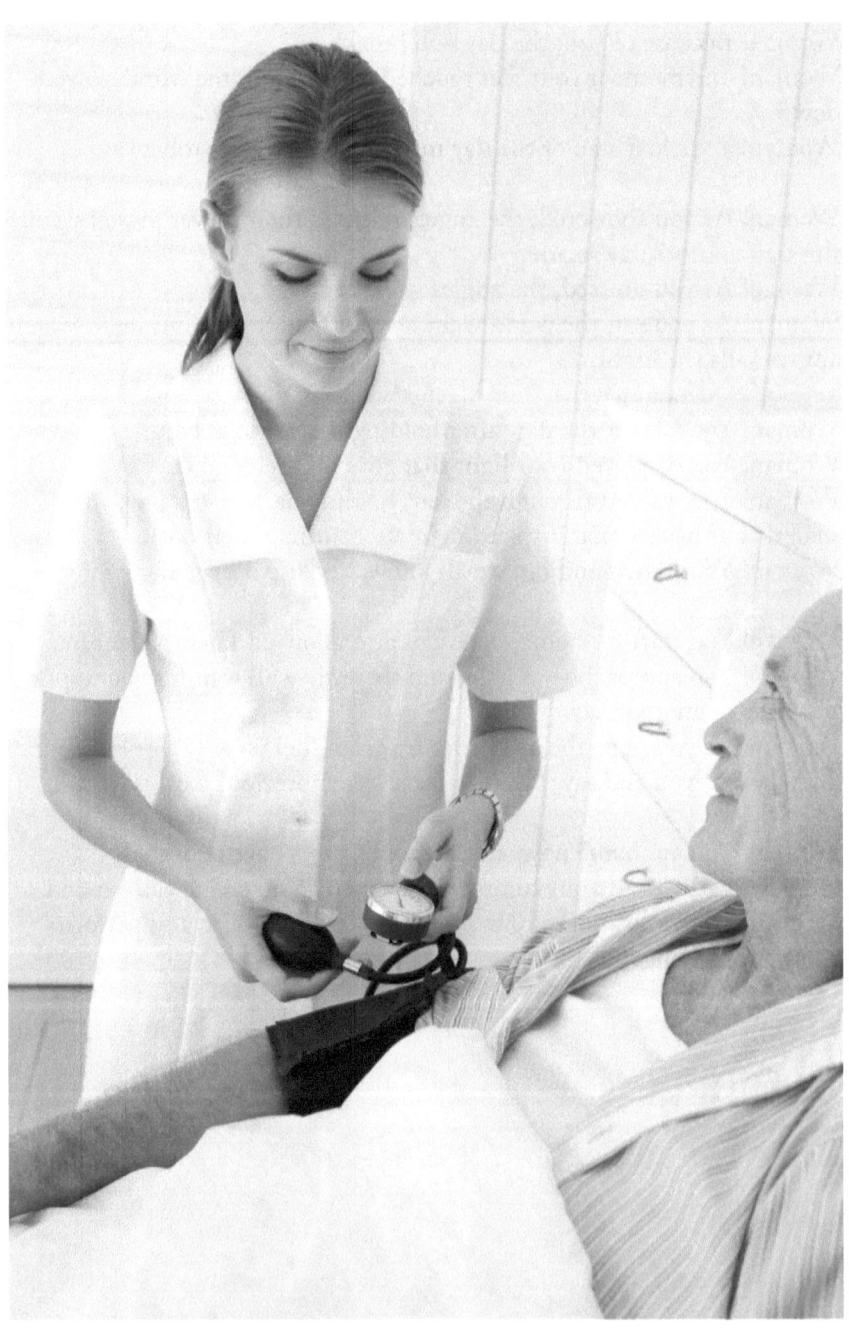

Women Nurses

What can a man say? You were there at day one, and you still are. We admired you then, and we still do. Our memories of you have caused us to get excited at your presence. We appreciate you from our heart. We remember how you comforted us and got us through the hard times at the doctor's office when we where little. It may have been a bump or a bruise, the cold or the flu, a broken bone or a stitch or two, but you were always there to pull us through.

Words cannot express our appreciation of you and all the wonderful and soothing things you do. We are thankful for your caring ways and your gift to the world. Your training is tough and your skills are exceptional, but your heart, commitment, and dedication are what won us over.

As we grow older, some of us desire to be with you for life. The men who have a special place with you are blessed.

The three types of nurses are

The Motherly One: She has been around for years. She is well respected and admired by her peers and patients. Her presence brings peace to any situation. Her advice is valued by all who know her.

The Happy One: She is always upbeat and excited about life. She is a pleasure to be around. She causes everyone to forget about their worries. Her smile brings life and light to all those in her presence. She is missed when she is not present.

The Sexy One: She is desirable! She knows it, her co-workers know it, and everyone who comes to the office knows it. She carries herself with grace and confidence. Whatever she wears, she makes sure it looks good on her. This is the one we think of as we leave the office and we look forward to seeing if we must return.

Women Nurses

Every man loves a nurse because your scent was there when we first came through and breathed the air.
Every man loves a nurse, believe it or not, we remember you washing us in that pot.
Every man loves a nurse, because we know it was you who wrapped us, fed us, and took care of us until Mom could too.

Every man appreciates the things you've done for us, back in the day, while Mom was finding her way.
Every man appreciates the memories you gave, how you would give us that pretty smile, which made us kick so wild.
Every man appreciates your being at the doctor's place; when Mom gave us to you, everything seemed to fit like a shoe.

As we grew older, we seemed to see you less and less.
But the memories of you were still packed in our sack.
As we grew older, we would see women who looked like you, sometimes in a TV show.
As we grew older, we developed a desire to hold you, to put you in our hands and mold you.

Every man loves the doctor's office, where we can see you in your hot uniform that makes us want to play the Congo drums.
Every man loves the doctor's office, where we can hear you call our name, which makes us forget all of our pain.
Every man loves the doctor's office because there we can see you in your true beauty, while you heal so many.

Every man longs to be with a nurse; because of the stories we've heard, we know you can make us fly like a bird.
Every man longs to be with a nurse because we understand why your smile made us kick so wild.
Every man longs to be with a nurse because you make us want to have a son, so he can experience your joy along his run.

Redheaded Women

Redheaded Women

You are indeed very rare! You stand out like a beautiful rose in the desert. You are a breath of fresh air on a hot sunny day. You are a drink of fresh water in the midst of a salty sea. You are indeed a rare, precious jewel that only two or three can pull!

Men have long wondered about you. In the past and even now, it seems that some of you have some doubt. It appears to us that you are not aware that you are a rare precious jewel. You are few, but that is the beauty of you.

Red is hot and fiery, just as we think you are. You can choose any man you desire and look good to him. Not many of us will turn down the opportunity to hold, cherish, and possess a rare and precious jewel such as yourself.

Rare: Extraordinary, exceptional, and remarkable.
Precious: Treasured, valuable, and important.
Jewel: Precious stone, crystal, or gem.

The redheaded woman is

A Rare and Precious Jewel: Nothing else need be said!

Redheaded Women

You, redheaded women, the stories we've heard about you make us want to fly like a bird.
You, redheaded women, you know you are rare; that's why every man is willing to take that dare.
You, redheaded women, the stories have been many; that's why men search for you like there aren't any.

You, redheaded women, how we wish that you were many, because for you, we'd stand against any.
You, redheaded women, when we look at your hair, it takes our minds to another time.
You, redheaded women, you are fair, which makes us want to stand next to you so bare.

You, redheaded women, it is so hard for us not to ask about some other parts.
You, redheaded women, who are not so many, like a precious jewel; only two or three men can pull.
You, redheaded women, so hot and tender, just the way any man likes it rendered.

You, redheaded women, without your fire to keep us free, where would all the men be?
You, redheaded women, we look at you so, and for you we'd break down any door.
You, redheaded women, I'll let you know before I close the door, we wish you were many, so we could defend you against any.

Military Women

Military Women

I am a veteran, and I remember the conversations we used to have about women in the military. You appeared to be so confident, strong, and sexy. You wore your uniforms so perfectly, and the way you walked made any man want to drop. You were well respected, yet greatly desired by us.

Why would a woman want to be a part of the military? What drives her? When did she start to dream of being a soldier? I would like to hear from such a woman. Military women have always been a mystery to us men, and I am sure many others would like to know as well.

Military Women

Every man wonders why you are here, willing to give your life so dear.
Strong, sexy, and determined, so attractive we want you to know.
Every man wonders, when he sees you for the first thunder, if he will be
the one to be next to you on the run.
Every man wonders if his plan is the one, enough to get you to want to
share his gun.

Every man knows, even in battles toe-to-toe, the inspiration you give
just being near him on the hill.
Every man knows, whether in peace or war, life or death, joy or pain, sun
or rain, there's nothing like having a woman there for everything.
Every man knows some of the fellows they have never had it better.
Being around you from day to day makes a man wish to never leave
Uncle Sam's way.

Every man loves it when you are dressed in uniform, marching your way
to the call of arms.
Every man loves it when we get to see you stand at attention.
We all know there's nothing better to see than your perfect being that
be.
Every man loves it when formation is over and the day has ended, for we
want to know if we can bring you some candy and maybe a little brandy.

To all the women in the military, I bow to honor you.
I give thanks and praise for the great sacrifice you've made.

Shy Women

Shy Women

It has been said that shy women are the ones you have to watch because you never can tell what's hidden underneath their shyness—that they are full of surprises and that they will take you places you've never dreamed of. Because of those words, men pay great attention to shy women. Men are attracted to shy women, and, in many situations, it appears that shy women find that hard to believe. Your shyness is one of the magnificent beauties of the world! It radiates desire, passion, and strength. And trust me! Men are drawn to desire, passion, and strength. It is like an addiction that many men will refuse to take an antidote for.

Your legend is what makes you a mystery. You don't have to do anything but be yourself. Your legend has paved the way for you. Enjoy it, have fun with it, and experiment with it. After all, it's *your* legend!

The Shy Woman: She exudes desire, passion, and strength. Her treasure is hidden deep beneath her shyness. She is perceived as difficult to approach, understand, and talk to. She is not aware that she is one of the magnificent beauties of the world. Men always have and always will seek for hidden treasure, for it is indeed one of our many quests. Know that we are constantly in pursuit of you. Smile!

Shy Women

Men see you; you can't hide.
We see you, though we may not see your eyes.
You walk around with your head hanging down, like you can't see all of us men around.
We see you and always wonder, what's underneath—your hidden thunder?

Men know what they say about shy women.
That deep inside you're more alive than any.
That's why men stare at you as though they're hypnotized and unable to recognize.
We mean you no harm; we're just pondering what hidden treasures are yonder.

Men are pondering whether or not they've just uncovered the jackpot.
For every man alive hunts daily for that very prize.
That hidden treasure, which makes him so special.
You are the mystery for us men that continually happens, again and again.

Men don't know how to get past your front door.
For many men know nothing of that which is called treasure-hunting.
If you would lift your head and show us your eyes, we could then see, how you've come to be.
We could then see what we need to be in order to see your treasure underneath.

You are a mystery, all men know.
But we want to be let into your den or given a passageway to your end.
Then we could say we hold the key to the greatest mystery above the sea.

Women in Heels

Women in Heels

What is the history of heels? Who designed them? What is the purpose of high heels?

I am sure the average man doesn't have a clue! Nevertheless, mighty and powerful are the heels when a woman slips them on. It seems as if the heel is a magical tool! It transforms a woman into pure desirability. They can bring a dead man who has lost his desire to life. They can real in the toughest of men if he is not careful. The very sound of a woman in heels can cause a shockwave in the middle of the desert! The heels are powerful with or without attire just as long as a woman is attached to them. Mighty and powerful are the heels!

There are many types of women in heels, but here are three that I believe are most noticeable:

The Educated One: She is aware of the added power that she has when she wears her heels. She enjoys the attention that she gets. She is friendly and smiles as she goes about her day. She knows that she is desired, but only entertains the men of her choice. Her walk is perfect, and she can move to any rhythm. She is pure beauty in motion that can't be denied.

The Naive One: She is unaware of the beauty and desire that heels can bring. Her walk is not polished. She is careless and stumbles through the day. Her heels may not fit properly. She would even prefer not to wear them. If she ever understands the power of the heels, she would be dangerous!

The Classy One: Her clothing is in alignment with her heels. Her undergarments are too. She is somewhat distant; she doesn't openly enjoy the fact that men desire her or is too clever to show it. When one thinks of rich in every aspect of the word, we think of this one. She knows how to dress and takes her time in the morning to make sure everything is where it should be. When she walks by there is only one word for a man to speak... damn!

Women in Heels

Men look fast when they hear the clicking of your heels, looking to see what beauty will be revealed.
Men look at you from head to toe, when they see you in heels, don't you know?
Men love a woman in heels, for it makes her sexier and so very real.

Men love women in heels because it makes her walk shift gears, smooth as butter and hypnotizing like no other.
Men love women in heels; tight jeans hugging her rear make us want to run and have a beer.
Men love women in heels, wearing a tight skirt and looking so alert, with legs that will make any man beg.

Men love women in heels; we like to see you in the store trying on more.
You look so sexy trying to find another pair; we are watching you with so much despair.
You slip them on, you slip them off, not aware of the men you've put in awe.

Women seem to know the power of the heel, for when you step out, your confidence is like an electric eel.
An electric eel? Yes! Because we'll feel a shock that stops us like a rock.
Heels, heels, heels, we are so thankful you made them real.
What excitement it brings and, at times, makes a man go insane.

My Daughter, Camille

As with me, so many men have experienced broken relationships that caused them and their offspring pain. I wrote this poem and dedicated this book to my daughter, Camille. I believe the words hold true for so many men who have children they love and, because of choices that were made, were not able to raise them.

To my daughter, Camille, you are awesome!

My Daughter, Camille

Lenisa Camille, you are such a thrill. I love you so, and wish to know you more.
When I see you, I see me; you have so much energy that needs to be free. I deeply regret not being there during your early years, to help you through and to share your tears too.

Your mother and I did not make it by. I still wonder at times, why? Why? Why?
Our divorce had nothing to do with you, even though it affected you too. Your mother is a great woman, for I see her in you. Forgive me if you are still hurting through and through.

You are an adult now, lovely, beautiful, and gracious too. I see how you make all the men go "Woo!" I've told you about men and their sin and how to not end up like a hen.
You've done well, and I'm so proud of you. You are a great woman who has a lot more to do.

My desire for you and me is to be close like a father and daughter should be.
My vision and goal from this day forth, is to have an excellent relationship with you.
What I rarely have said to you, my dear, and shame on me, for I've shed a tear.

I love you, Lenisa Camille! I always have, and I always will!

Dad